I0508799

This Book belongs to

____

____

____

www.ingramcontent.com/pod-product-compliance
Lightning Source LLC
Chambersburg PA
CBHW030947240526
45463CB00016B/1987